Delights and Warnings: 4

# Magic and Mystery

poems selected by
John and Gillian Beer

illustrated by
Giovanni Caselli

MACDONALD EDUCATIONAL

# About the poems

Poetry and magic have always been closely linked. Some of the earliest poems of all were charms and magic spells. Words with a rhythm or rhyme are much easier to remember, so important pieces of knowledge were often passed on in that way.

People remembered **Charms** against things that came mysteriously, like burns or hiccups.

The fact that they were in rhyme and had a rhythm gave them a sort of power. They seemed to *mean* more, because the rhymes held unexpected things together.

Other verses give magic to ordinary life by suggesting that days of the week, or colours, have a meaning of their own. The fishermen enjoy the thought of coming home for the weekend and make a rhyme about the different days. Can you make a rhyme like that about the days of the school week?

Warts are another of the mysterious things that happen to our bodies. They are harmless, but nobody likes having them and the poem **Warts** tells us about ways in which people try to make them go away.

There is always something magical about having knowledge that other people don't have, and also about getting hold of it. That is why we all enjoy riddles.

The **Riddles** given here are from *The Hobbit* by J. R. R. Tolkien, and are about things that are still important to us. Can you solve them? The illustration next to each one will give you a clue to the answer. In *The Hobbit* the riddles are part of a life-or-death contest, where the one who fails to answer the other's riddle will fall into his power.

In **The False Knight upon the Road** much the same is happening. The small boy on his way to school meets a knight who tries to frighten him with threatening questions, but each time the boy has a good answer ready—just as the rider has in **O where are you going?**

The next poem, **I saw a Peacock**, is one long riddle: does it take any of the magic away when you know the answer? There are no answers to the riddles in **Ariel Sings**—does this make it more magical?

Although magic often goes with power, Ben Jonson's poem **It is not Growing like a Tree** is a reminder that small and perfect things can sometimes be the most magical.

Now read **Kubla Khan** aloud in a slow, chanting voice. See how this gives the poem a sense of power and mystery. Try drawing the scene in the poem and then ask your friends to do the same. You will find how many ways there are of seeing it, and how there is no 'right' one.

Sometimes wonder comes from seeing something unexpectedly, or in an unusual light. Imagine yourself as the Indian in **The Discovery**. Or think how it would be to come into **Nottamun Town**. Why do you think the riddles at the end of this poem are so very difficult?

So long as our imaginations are alive, there is always some magic in the world. Listen to the wind from your bedroom and you will know what Robert Louis Stevenson means in **Windy Nights**. And although none of us has ever experienced what happens in **Unwelcome**, we all know what it would be like.

Reading Wallace Stevens' poem **Ploughing on Sunday** after **Unwelcome** is rather like waking up after a bad dream and seeing how beautiful the world is after all. Many poets would not use some of the words he uses, like 'Tum-ti-tum', for fear of sounding childish, but Stevens knows that some things feel magically the same whether you are a small child or a grown-up. T.E. Hulme, in **Autumn**, too, knows that magic is always present in our lives. Does is make the stars seem ordinary to say that they are like town children, or more magical? What does it do to the moon to say it is like a forgotten balloon?

The moon is often associated with magic, partly because of its strange light and partly because of its mysterious effect on the natural world—especially the sea. People tell stories about it; they picture a moon-goddess, or 'the man in the moon'; or, like the Japanese poet who wrote **The Hare in the Moon**, they see a hare and imagine how it got there.

Judith Wright in **Full Moon Rhyme** turns this idea around, by making all the dogs who howl at the moon do so because they too see a hare in it; and in **Moon-Wind** Ted Hughes paints a strange and rather eerie picture of the kind of wind you might find on the moon.

A feeling of strangeness can come from doing something quite ordinary like climbing a hill, and seeing how small the world suddenly looks (**High on the Hill**). Or from imagining countries we have never been to, as Robert Louis Stevenson does in **Travel**.

But when you actually go to a strange country you may still have a feeling that the magic is a little further on—like the American in another state who imagines that the true place to be is **Idaho**.

Two of the last poems are 'chain poems' in which everything connects to something else until you end up with some quite unexpected connection.

The Indians of **Aztec Song** might not find this as surprising as we do, because they feel closer to the earth than modern man does.

There's something more like a detective story in **This is the Key**, where we half expect to find at the end that we have discovered the key to a mystery. The key we find, however, is the same one that the Aztec Indians know: it is a key to life itself.

The boy in **Is this all?** on the other hand cannot find any mystery or excitement in his life. Do you sympathize with him? Any why do you think his mother smiles?

There is just a touch of the sinister about the last poem, but there is a good deal more of delight. Imagine a Christmas morning on which you never got to the end of unwrapping your presents. **Warning to Children** has something of the same magic, and it also helps to explain why all of us enjoy poems that have some sort of mystery about them—and how good poetry can be at expressing that mystery.

## RIDDLES

Voiceless it cries,
Wingless flutters,
Toothless bites,
Mouthless mutters.

What has roots as nobody sees,
Is taller than trees
    Up, up it goes,
    And yet never grows?

It cannot be seen, cannot be felt,
Cannot be heard, cannot be smelt.
It lies behind stars and under hills,
    And empty holes it fills.
It comes first and follows after,
    Ends life, kills laughter.

Alive without breath,
As cold as death;
Never thirsty, ever drinking,
All in mail never clinking.

Thirty white horses on a red hill,
First they champ,
Then they stamp,
Then they stand still.

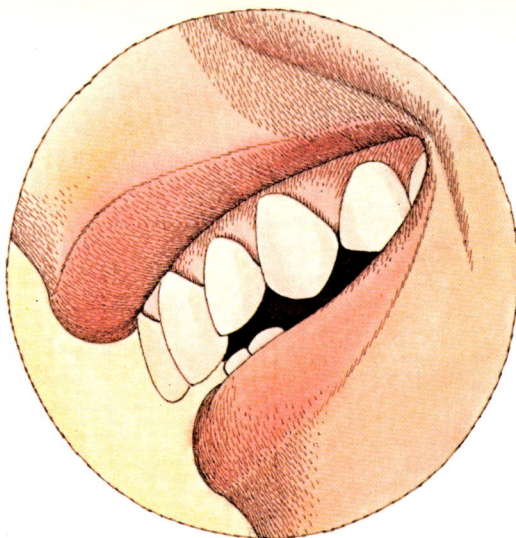

An eye in a blue face
Saw an eye in a green face.
'That eye is like to this eye'
Said the first eye,
'But in low place
Not in high place.'

A box without hinges, key, or lid,
Yet golden treasure inside is hid.

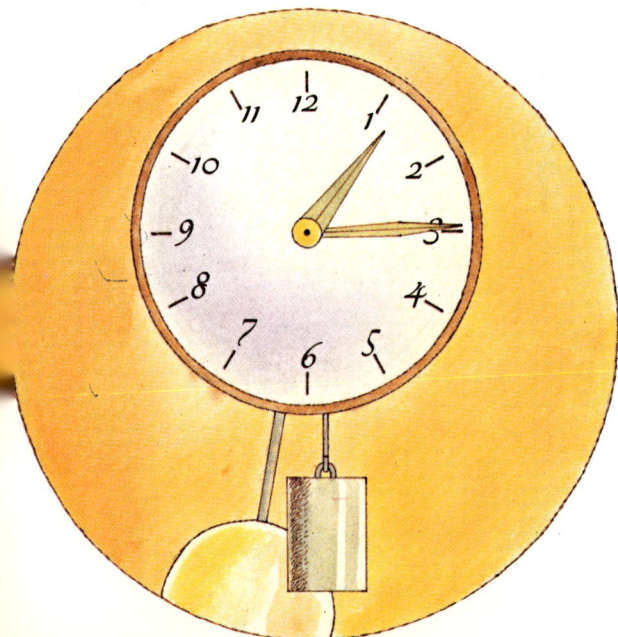

This thing all things devours:
Birds, beasts, trees, flowers;
Gnaws iron, bites steel;
Grinds hard stones to meal;
Slays king, ruins town,
And beats high mountain down.

J. R. R. TOLKIEN

## CHARMS

Hickup, hickup, go away,
Come again another day:
Hickup, hickup, when I bake,
I'll give to you a butter-cake.

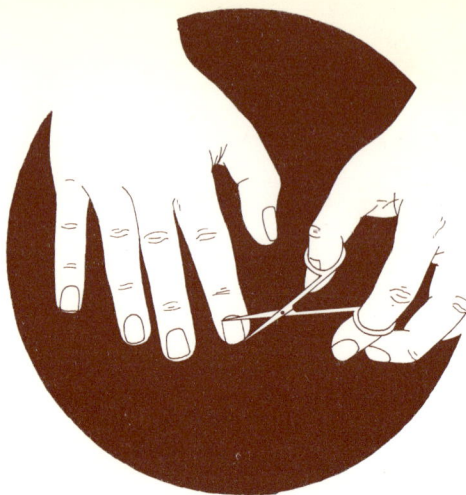

Blue is true,
Yellow's jealous,
Green's forsaken,
Red's brazen,
White is love,
And black is death!

Cut them on Monday, you cut them for health;
Cut them on Tuesday, you cut them for wealth;
Cut them on Wednesday, you cut them for news;
Cut them on Thursday, a new pair of shoes;
Cut them on Friday, you cut them for sorrow;
Cut them on Saturday, see your true love
 tomorrow;
Cut them on Sunday, the devil will be with you
 all the week.

Two angels from the north,
One brought fire, the other brought frost:
 Out fire!
 In frost!
In the name of the Father, Son, and Holy Ghost.

Today is silver Saturday,
The morn's the resting day,
Monday up and to it again,
And Tuesday, push away.

## WARTS

You can sell them for a penny to
your mother

                                    or

You can tie knots for each one
in a piece of string
and plant it at the bottom of your garden
and water it
every morning
that makes them grow under the earth

                                    or

You can have them charmed
if you know a charmer
there are lots in Cornwall you must
leave her a gift and not say thankyou
then she will sing
an incantation

                                    or

there is the witches way.
You take a special white round stone
for every one
and put them in a pretty red bag
throw it over your shoulder
into the middle of the road —

*Don't touch that bag it's got
warts in it*

                                    or

If you can find the green toad you
got them from you can
give them back to him if he'll have them

                                    or

You can rub snails on them or slugs
and if that doesn't cure them

you still want them

                        JENI COUZYN
        '*The Soul is the Breath in your Body*'

# THE FALSE KNIGHT UPON
# THE ROAD

'O where are you going?'
*Quoth the false knight upon the road:*
'I'm going to school.'
*Quoth the wee boy, and still he stood.*

'What is that upon your back?'
*Quoth the false knight upon the road:*
'Why, sure it is my books.'
*Quoth the wee boy, and still he stood.*

'What is that you've got in your arm?'
*Quoth the false knight upon the road:*
'Why sure it is my peat.'[1]
*Quoth the wee boy, and still he stood.*

'Whose are those sheep?'
*Quoth the false knight upon the road:*
'They're mine and my mother's.'
*Quoth the wee boy, and still he stood.*

'How many of them are mine?'
*Quoth the false knight upon the road:*
'All them that have blue tails.'
*Quoth the wee boy, and still he stood.*

'I wish you were on yon tree.'
*Quoth the false knight upon the road:*
'And a good ladder under me.'
*Quoth the wee boy, and still he stood.*

'And the ladder for to break.'
*Quoth the false knight upon the road:*
'And *you* for to fall down.'
*Quoth the wee boy, and still he stood.*

'I wish you were in yon sea.'
*Quoth the false knight upon the road:*
'And a good boat under me.'
*Quoth the wee boy, and still he stood,*

'And the boat for to break.'
*Quoth the false knight on the road:*
'And *you* to be drowned.'
*Quoth the wee boy, and still he stood.*

[1] Peat for the school fire.

# 'O WHERE ARE YOU GOING?'

'O where are you going?' said reader to rider,
'That valley is fatal when furnaces burn,
Yonder's the midden whose odours will madden,
That gap is the grave where the tall return.'

'O do you imagine,' said fearer to farer,
'That dusk will delay on your path to the pass,
Your diligent looking discover the lacking
Your footsteps feel from granite to grass?'

'O what was that bird,' said horror to hearer,
'Did you see that shape in the twisted trees?
Behind you swiftly the figure comes softly,
The spot on your skin is a shocking disease.'

'Out of this house'—said rider to reader,
'Yours never will'—said farer to fearer,
'They're looking for you'—said hearer to horror,
As he left them there, as he left them there.

W. H. AUDEN

## I SAW A PEACOCK WITH A FIERY TAIL

I saw a Peacock with a fiery tail,
I saw a blazing Comet drop down hail,
I saw a Cloud with ivy circled round,
I saw a sturdy Oak creep on the ground,
I saw a Pismire swallow up a whale,
I saw a raging Sea brim full of ale,
I saw a Venice Glass sixteen foot deep,
I saw a Well full of men's tears that weep,
I saw their Eyes all in a flame of fire,
I saw a House as big as the moon and higher,
I saw the Sun even in the midst of night,
I saw the Man that saw this wondrous sight.

*(To solve the riddle, read from the middle of the first line to the middle of the next, and so on through the poem)*

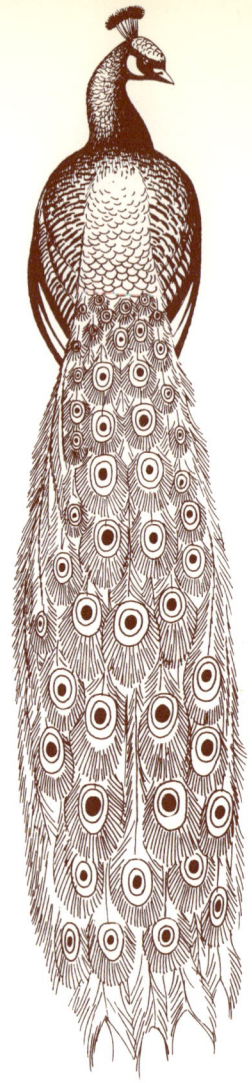

## ARIEL SINGS

Full fathom five thy father lies;
  Of his bones are coral made;
Those are pearls that were his eyes:
  Nothing of him that doth fade,
But doth suffer a sea-change
Into something rich and strange.
Sea-nymphs hourly ring his knell:
      *(Chorus:)* Ding-dong bell.

WILLIAM SHAKESPEARE
*The Tempest*

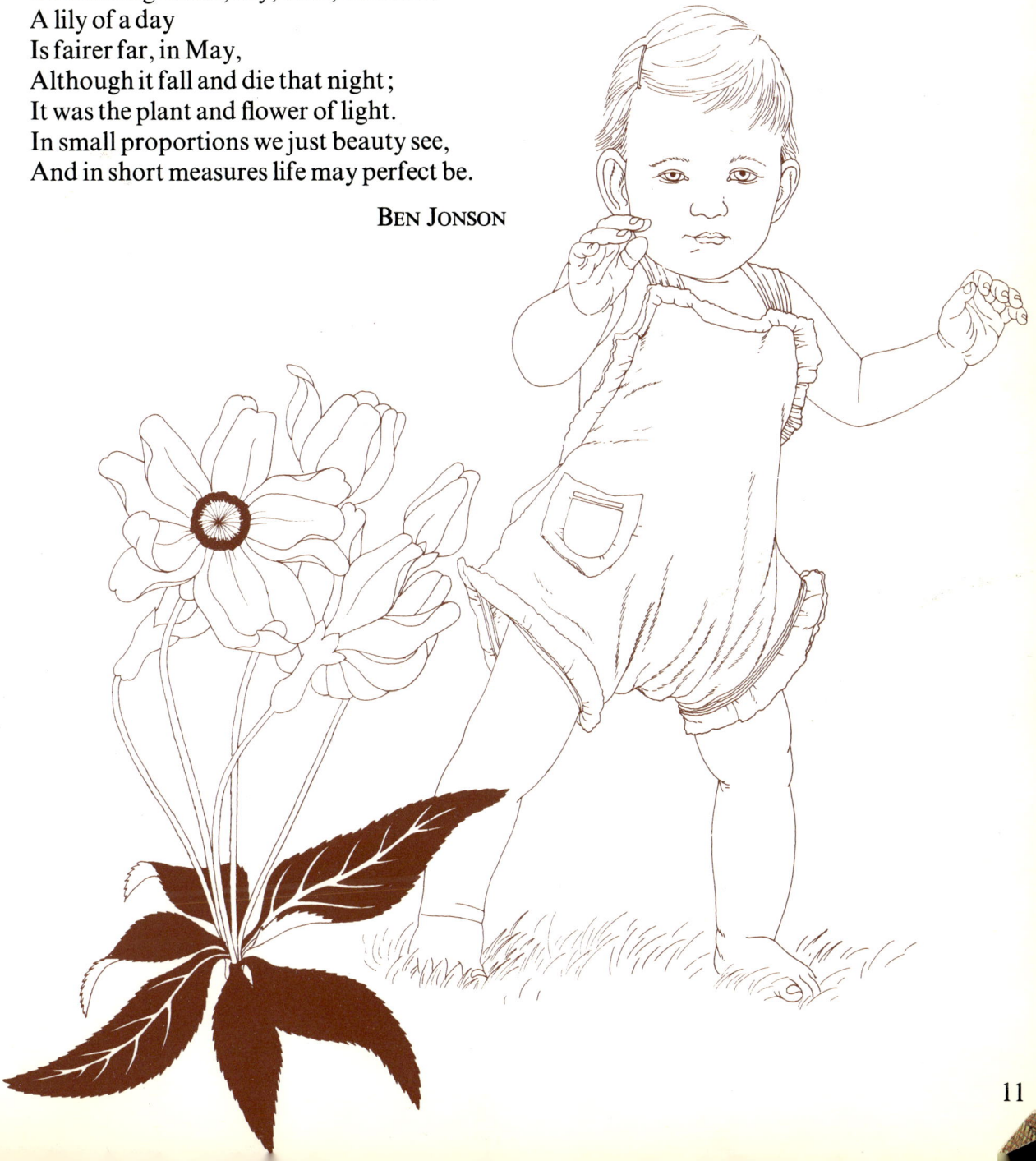

## IT IS NOT GROWING LIKE A TREE . . .

It is not growing like a tree
In bulk, doth make man better be;
Or standing long an oak, three hundred year,
To fall a log at last, dry, bald, and sere:
A lily of a day
Is fairer far, in May,
Although it fall and die that night;
It was the plant and flower of light.
In small proportions we just beauty see,
And in short measures life may perfect be.

BEN JONSON

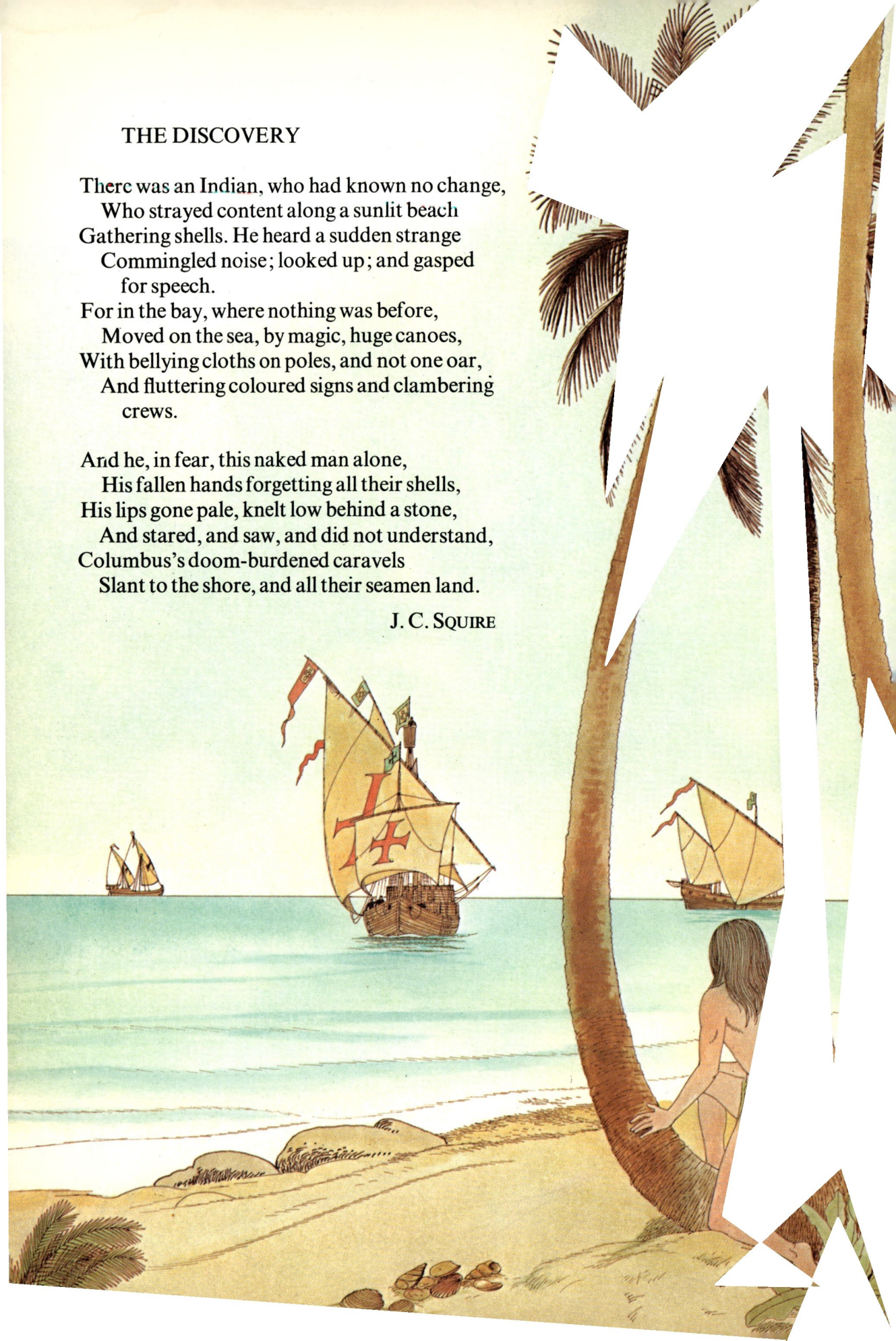

# THE DISCOVERY

There was an Indian, who had known no change,
   Who strayed content along a sunlit beach
Gathering shells. He heard a sudden strange
   Commingled noise; looked up; and gasped
     for speech.
For in the bay, where nothing was before,
   Moved on the sea, by magic, huge canoes,
With bellying cloths on poles, and not one oar,
   And fluttering coloured signs and clambering
     crews.

And he, in fear, this naked man alone,
   His fallen hands forgetting all their shells,
His lips gone pale, knelt low behind a stone,
   And stared, and saw, and did not understand,
Columbus's doom-burdened caravels
   Slant to the shore, and all their seamen land.

J. C. SQUIRE

## NOTTAMUN TOWN

In Nottamun Town not a soul would look up,
Not a soul would look up, not a soul would
   look down,
Not a soul would look up, not a soul would
   look down
To tell me the way to Nottamun Town.

I rode a big horse that was called a grey mare,
Grey mane and tail, grey stripes down his back,
Grey mane and tail, grey stripes down his back,
There weren't a hair on him but what was
   called black.

She stood so still, she threw me to the dirt,
She tore my hide and bruised my shirt;
From stirrup to stirrup, I mounted again
And on my ten toes I rode over the plain.

Met the King and the Queen and a company
   of men
A-walking behind and a-riding before.
A stark naked drummer came walking along
With his hands in his bosom a-beating his drum.

Sat down on a hot and cold frozen stone
Ten thousand stood round me and I was alone.
Took my heart in my hand to keep my head warm.
Ten thousand got drowned that never were born.

## KUBLA KHAN

In Xanadu did Kubla Khan
A stately pleasure-dome decree:
Where Alph, the sacred river, ran
Through caverns measureless to man
    Down to a sunless sea.
So twice five miles of fertile ground
With walls and towers were girdled round:
And here were gardens bright with sinuous rills,
Where blossomed many an incense-bearing tree;
And here were forests ancient as the hills,
Enfolding sunny spots of greenery.

But oh! that deep romantic chasm which slanted
Down the green hill athwart a cedarn cover!
A savage place! as holy and enchanted
As e'er beneath a waning moon was haunted
By woman wailing for her demon-lover!
And from this chasm, with ceaseless turmoil
    seething,
As if this earth in fast thick pants were breathing,
A mighty fountain momently was forced:
Amid whose swift half-intermitted burst
Huge fragments vaulted like rebounding hail,
Or chaffy grain beneath the thresher's flail:
And 'mid these dancing rocks at once and ever
It flung up momently the sacred river.
Five miles meandering with a mazy motion
Through wood and dale the sacred river ran,
Then reached the caverns measureless to man,
And sank in tumult to a lifeless ocean:
And 'mid this tumult Kubla heard from far
Ancestral voices prophesying war!

    The shadow of the dome of pleasure
    Floated midway on the waves;
    Where was heard the mingled measure
    From the fountain and the caves.
It was a miracle of rare device,
A sunny pleasure-dome with caves of ice!

    A damsel with a dulcimer
    In a vision once I saw:
    It was an Abyssinian maid,

And on her dulcimer she played,
Singing of Mount Abora.
Could I revive within me
Her symphony and song,
To such a deep delight 'twould win me,
That with music loud and long,
I would build that dome in air,
That sunny dome! those caves of ice!
And all who heard should see them there,
And all should cry, Beware! Beware!
His flashing eyes, his floating hair!
Weave a circle round him thrice,
And close your eyes with holy dread,
For he on honey-dew hath fed,
And drunk the milk of Paradise.

S. T. COLERIDGE

# WINDY NIGHTS

Whenever the moon and stars are set,
   Whenever the wind is high,
All night long in the dark and wet,
   A man goes riding by.
Late in the night when the fires are out,
Why does he gallop and gallop about?

Whenever the trees are crying aloud,
   And ships are tossed at sea,
By, on the highway, low and loud,
   By at the gallop goes he.
By at the gallop he goes, and then
By he comes back at the gallop again.

ROBERT LOUIS STEVENSON

# UNWELCOME

We were young, we were merry, we were very very wise,
    And the door stood open at our feast,
When there passed us a woman with the West in her eyes,
    And a man with his back to the East.

O, still grew the hearts that were beating so fast,
    The loudest voice was still.
The jest died away on our lips as they passed,
    And the rays of July struck chill.

The cups of red wine turned pale on the board,
    The white bread black as soot.
The hound forgot the hand of her lord,
    She fell down at his foot.

Low let me die, where the dead dog lies,
    Ere I sit me down again at a feast,
When there passes a woman with the West in her eyes,
    And a man with his back to the East.

MARY COLERIDGE

## PLOUGHING ON SUNDAY

The white cock's tail
Tosses in the wind.
The turkey-cock's tail
Glitters in the sun.

Water in the fields.
The wind pours down.
The feathers flare
And bluster in the wind.

Remus, blow your horn!
I'm ploughing on Sunday,
Ploughing North America.
Blow your horn!

Tum-ti-tum,
Ti-tum-tum-tum!
The turkey-cock's tail
Spreads to the sun.

The white cock's tail
Streams to the moon.
Water in the fields.
The wind pours down.

WALLACE STEVENS

18

## ABOVE THE DOCK

Above the quiet dock in midnight,
Tangled in the tall mast's corded height,
Hangs the moon. What seemed so far away
Is but a child's balloon, forgotten after play.

T. E. HULME

## AUTUMN

A touch of cold in the Autumn night—
I walked abroad,
And saw the ruddy moon lean over a hedge
Like a red-faced farmer.
I did not stop to speak, but nodded,
And round about were the wistful stars
With white faces like town children.

T. E. HULME

# FULL MOON RHYME

There's a hare in the moon tonight,
crouching alone in the bright
buttercup field of the moon;
and all the dogs in the world
howl at the hare in the moon.

'I chased that hare to the sky,'
the hungry dogs all cry.
'The hare jumped into the moon
and left me here in the cold.
I chased that hare to the moon.'

'Come down again, wild hare.
We can see you there,'
the dogs all howl to the moon.
'Come down again to the world,
you mad black hare in the moon,

'or we will grow wings and fly
up to the star-grassed sky
to hunt you out of the moon,'
the hungry dogs of the world
howl at the hare in the moon.

JUDITH WRIGHT

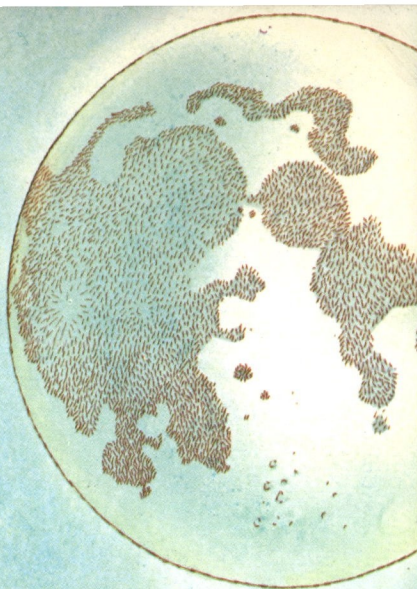

# THE HARE IN THE MOON

Long long ago, they say,
Lived a monkey, a hare, and a fox.
Together they formed a bond
Of friendship:
In the day, they romped
In the hills and fields,
At night, to their
Forest they returned.
And so time passed,
Until the god who lives
In the eternal heavens
Heard the story.
'But is it true?'
He asked, and turned himself
Into an old man,
Teetering along to see.
There he found them
Just as he had heard,
Romping and playing,
Their hearts made one.
Resting his limbs awhile,
Pausing to get his breath,
He threw away his staff
And shouted, 'Help me!
Help a hungry old man!'
'That's not hard,' they said,
And then, quick as a flash,
From the copse behind
The monkey gathered berries;
From the river bank in front
The fox snapped up a fish,
But the hare, hopping
All about the place,
Did not a thing to help.
'Oh! that hare—his idea's
Always different,' they cursed.
But all to no good. Then,
'Break these twigs,' said monkey,
'Light a fire,' said fox.
Hare did as he was told.
And then, into the smoke
And flames they hurled him,
And served him up to
The old man, all unwitting.

He, lifting his eyes
To the heavens that last for ever,
Sobbed and wept and then
Rolled prostrate on the ground.
Soon, beating on his breast,
He asked, 'Which of the three,
These three old friends, which
Treated me the best?
They were all kind.' And yet,
Thinking that the hare
Was the finest of them all,
He took him, dead,
And cast him high up
To the palace of the moon
In the heavens that last for ever.

RYŌKAN

# THE WITCHES' CHARM

The owl is abroad, the bat and the toad,
　And so is the cat-o'-mountain;
The ant and the mole sit both in a hole,
　And frog peeps out o' the fountain;
The dogs they do bay, and the timbrels play,
　The spindle is now a-turning;
The moon it is red, and the stars are fled,
　But all the sky is a-burning:
The ditch is made, and our nails the spade,
With pictures full, of wax and of wool;
Their livers I stick with needles quick:
That lacks but the blood, to make up the flood.
　Quickly, dame, then, bring your part in,
　Spur, spur upon little Martin,
　Merrily, merrily, make him sail,
　A worm in his mouth, and a thorn in's tail,
　Fire above and fire below,
　With a whip i' your hand to make him go.
　Oh, now she's come!
　Let all be dumb.

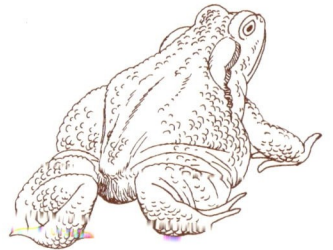

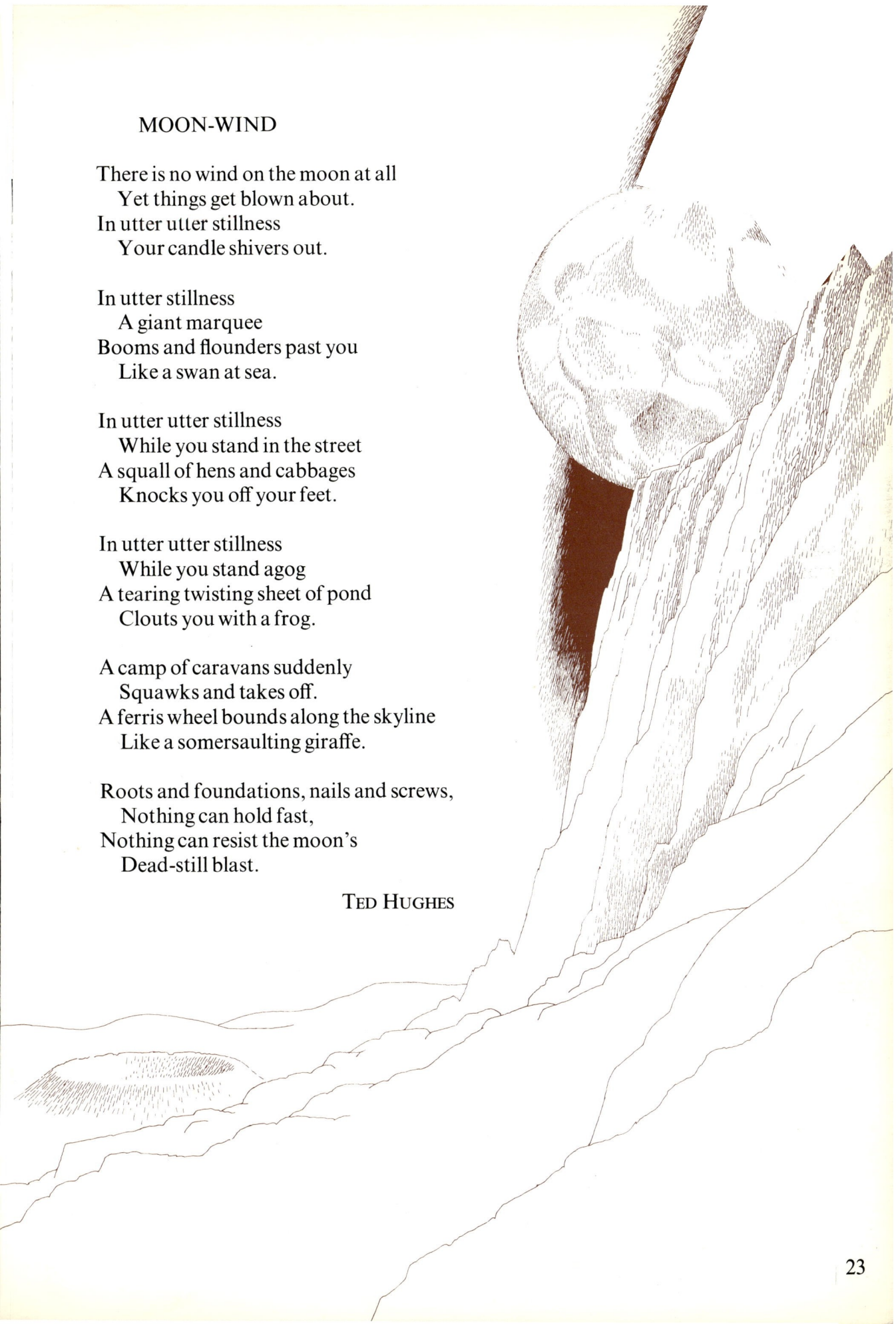

## MOON-WIND

There is no wind on the moon at all
   Yet things get blown about.
In utter utter stillness
   Your candle shivers out.

In utter stillness
   A giant marquee
Booms and flounders past you
   Like a swan at sea.

In utter utter stillness
   While you stand in the street
A squall of hens and cabbages
   Knocks you off your feet.

In utter utter stillness
   While you stand agog
A tearing twisting sheet of pond
   Clouts you with a frog.

A camp of caravans suddenly
   Squawks and takes off.
A ferris wheel bounds along the skyline
   Like a somersaulting giraffe.

Roots and foundations, nails and screws,
   Nothing can hold fast,
Nothing can resist the moon's
   Dead-still blast.

TED HUGHES

## TRAVEL

I should like to rise and go
Where the golden apples grow;
Where below another sky
Parrot islands anchored lie,
And, watched by cockatoos and goats,
Lonely Crusoes building boats;
Where in sunshine reaching out
Eastern cities, miles about,
Are with mosque and minaret
Among sandy gardens set,
And the rich goods from near and far
Hang for sale in the bazaar;
Where the Great Wall round China goes,
And on one side the desert blows,
And with bell and voice and drum,
Cities on the other hum;
Where are forests, hot as fire,
Wide as England, tall as a spire,
Full of apes and coconuts
And the negro hunters' huts;
Where the knotty crocodile
Lies and blinks in the Nile,
And the red flamingo flies
Hunting fish before his eyes;

Where in jungles, near and far,
Man-devouring tigers are,
Lying close and giving ear
Lest the hunt be drawing near,
Or a comer-by be seen
Swinging in a palanquin;
Where among the desert sands
Some deserted city stands,
All its children, sweep and prince,
Grown to manhood ages since,
Not a foot in street or house,
Not a stir of child or mouse,
And when kindly falls the night,
In all the town no spark of light.
There I'll come when I'm a man
With a camel caravan;
Light a fire in the gloom
Of some dusty dining-room;
See the pictures on the walls,
Heroes, fights and festivals;
And in a corner find the toys
Of the old Egyptian boys.

ROBERT LOUIS STEVENSON

## HIGH ON THE HILL

High on the hill I can see it all,
the anthill men and the doll's house town,
the bowl of sea and the trim toy ships.
Here only the trees at hand are tall.

High on the hill I can touch a cloud
or measure miles with my fingertips,
can hide the town with a palm turned down
and drown its noise when I speak aloud.

High on the hill it's all a joke
and I wonder why I bothered at all
with the clockwork cars and the anthill folk
that height and distance make so small.

TOM WRIGHT

26

## THERE WAS A NAUGHTY BOY . . .

There was a naughty Boy,
  And a naughty Boy was he,
He ran away to Scotland
  The people for to see —
    There he found
    That the ground
    Was as hard,
    That a yard
    Was as long,
    That a song
    Was as merry,
    That a cherry
    Was as red—
    That lead
    Was as weighty,
    That fourscore
    Was as eighty,
    That a door
    Was as wooden
    As in England—
    So he stood in
    His shoes
    And he wonder'd,
    He wonder'd,
    He stood in his
    Shoes and he wonder'd . . .

JOHN KEATS

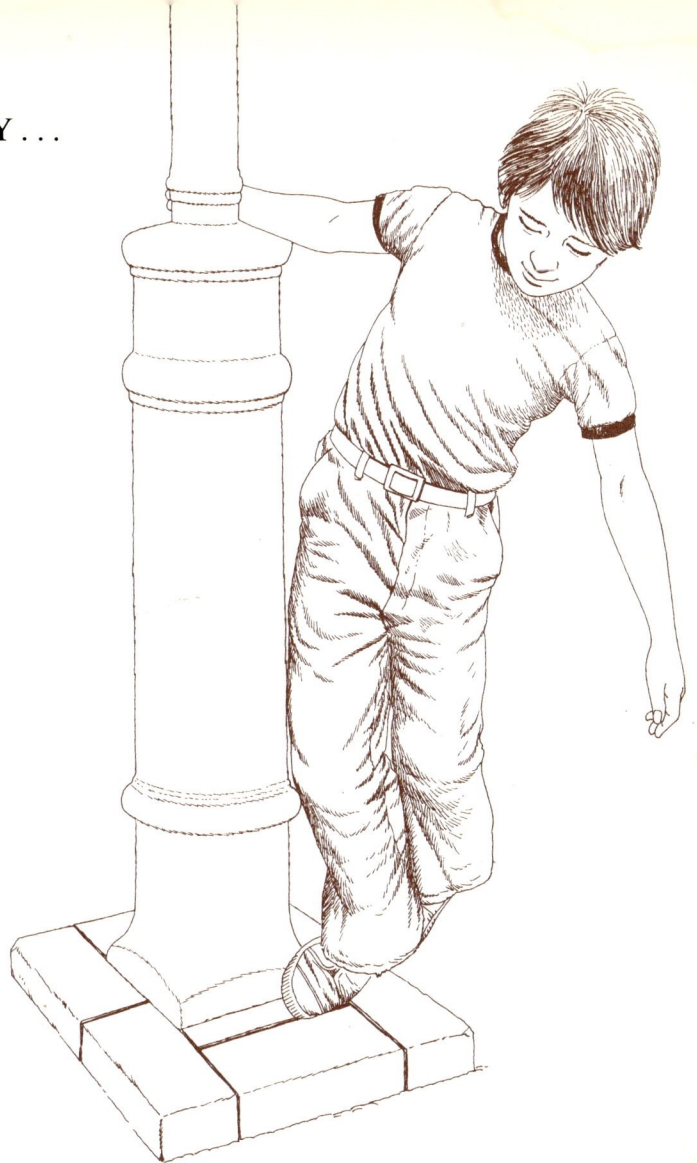

## AUNTIE'S SKIRTS

Whenever Auntie moves around,
Her dresses make a curious sound;
They trail behind her up the floor,
And trundle after through the door.

ROBERT LOUIS STEVENSON

## IDAHO

They say there is a land
  Where crystal waters flow,
Where veins of purest gold are found
  Way out in Idaho.

We'll need no pick or spade,
  No shovel, pan or hoe,
The largest chunks are on the ground
  Way out in Idaho.

## AZTEC SONG

we only came to sleep
we only came to dream
it is not true
no it is not true
that we came to live on the earth

we are changed into the grass of springtime
our hearts will grow green again
and they will open their petals
but our body is like a rose tree
    it puts forth flowers and then withers

*Nahuatl Indians, Mexico*
*translated by* LOWELL DUNHAM

## THIS IS THE KEY

This is the Key of the Kingdom
In that Kingdom is a city;
In that city is a town;
In that town there is a street;
In that street there winds a lane;
In that lane there is a yard;
In that yard there is a house;
In that house there waits a room;
In that room an empty bed;
And on that bed a basket—
A Basket of Sweet Flowers:
    Of Flowers, of Flowers;
    A Basket of Sweet Flowers.

Flowers in a Basket;
Basket on the bed;
Bed in the chamber;
Chamber in the house;
House in the weedy yard;
Yard in the winding lane;
Lane in the broad street;
Street in the high town;
Town in the city;
City in the Kingdom—
This is the Key of the Kingdom;
    Of the Kingdom this is the Key.

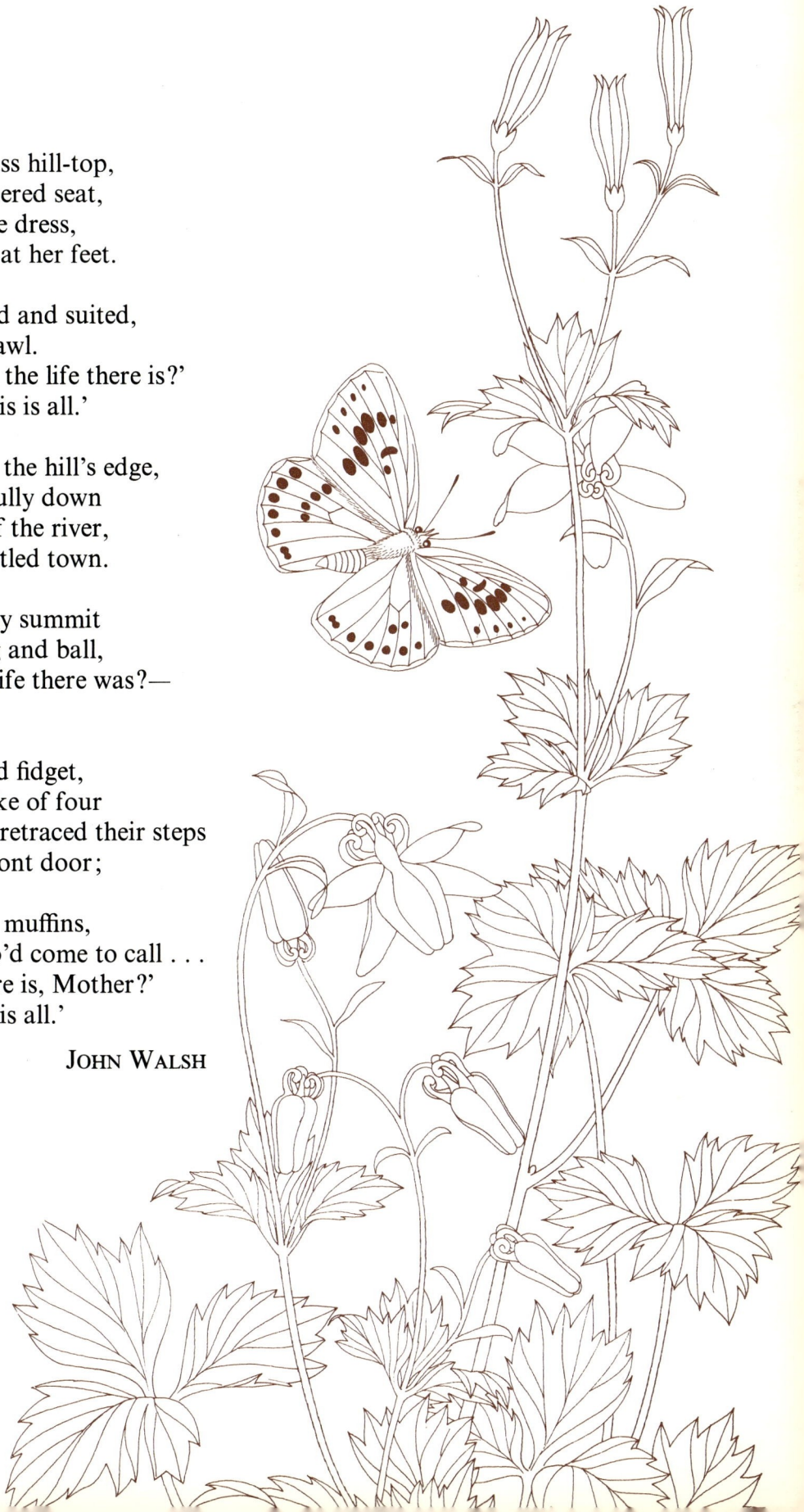

## IS THIS ALL?

High on the short-grass hill-top,
By the green and blistered seat,
Mother sat in her blue dress,
And Towser, flopped at her feet.

And near them, hatted and suited,
Father in Sunday sprawl.
Bob asked, 'Is this all the life there is?'
Said Mother, 'Yes, this is all.'

Bob walked across to the hill's edge,
And looked thoughtfully down
At the muddy twist of the river,
At the roofed and castled town.

To climb to this grassy summit
With parents and dog and ball,
Could this be all the life there was?—
Could this be all?

And then to stand and fidget,
Till sharp on the stroke of four
The parents rose and retraced their steps
Down to their own front door;

To a Sunday tea with muffins,
And the Pollards who'd come to call . . .
'Is this all the life there is, Mother?'
Mother smiled. 'This is all.'

JOHN WALSH

## WARNING TO CHILDREN

Children, if you dare to think
Of the greatness, rareness, muchness,
Fewness of this precious only
Endless world in which you say
You live, you think of things like this:
Blocks of slate enclosing dappled
Red and green, enclosing tawny
Yellow nets, enclosing white
And black acres of dominoes,
Where a neat brown paper parcel
Tempts you to untie the string.
In the parcel a small island,
On the island a large tree,
On the tree a husky fruit.
Strip the husk and pare the rind off:
In the kernel you will see
Blocks of slate enclosed by dappled
Red and green, enclosed by tawny
Yellow nets, enclosed by white
And black acres of dominoes,
Where the same brown paper parcel—
Children, leave the string alone!
For who dares undo the parcel
Finds himself at once inside it,
On the island, in the fruit,
Blocks of slate about his head,
Finds himself enclosed by dappled
Green and red, enclosed by yellow
Tawny nets, enclosed by black
And white acres of dominoes,
With the same brown paper parcel
Still unopened on his knee.
And, if he then should dare to think
Of the fewness, muchness, rareness,
Greatness of this endless only
Precious world in which he says
He lives—he then unties the string.

ROBERT GRAVES

32

# Delights and Warnings: 2

# Taking a closer look

poems selected by
John and Gillian Beer

illustrated by
Giovanni Caselli

MACDONALD EDUCATIONAL

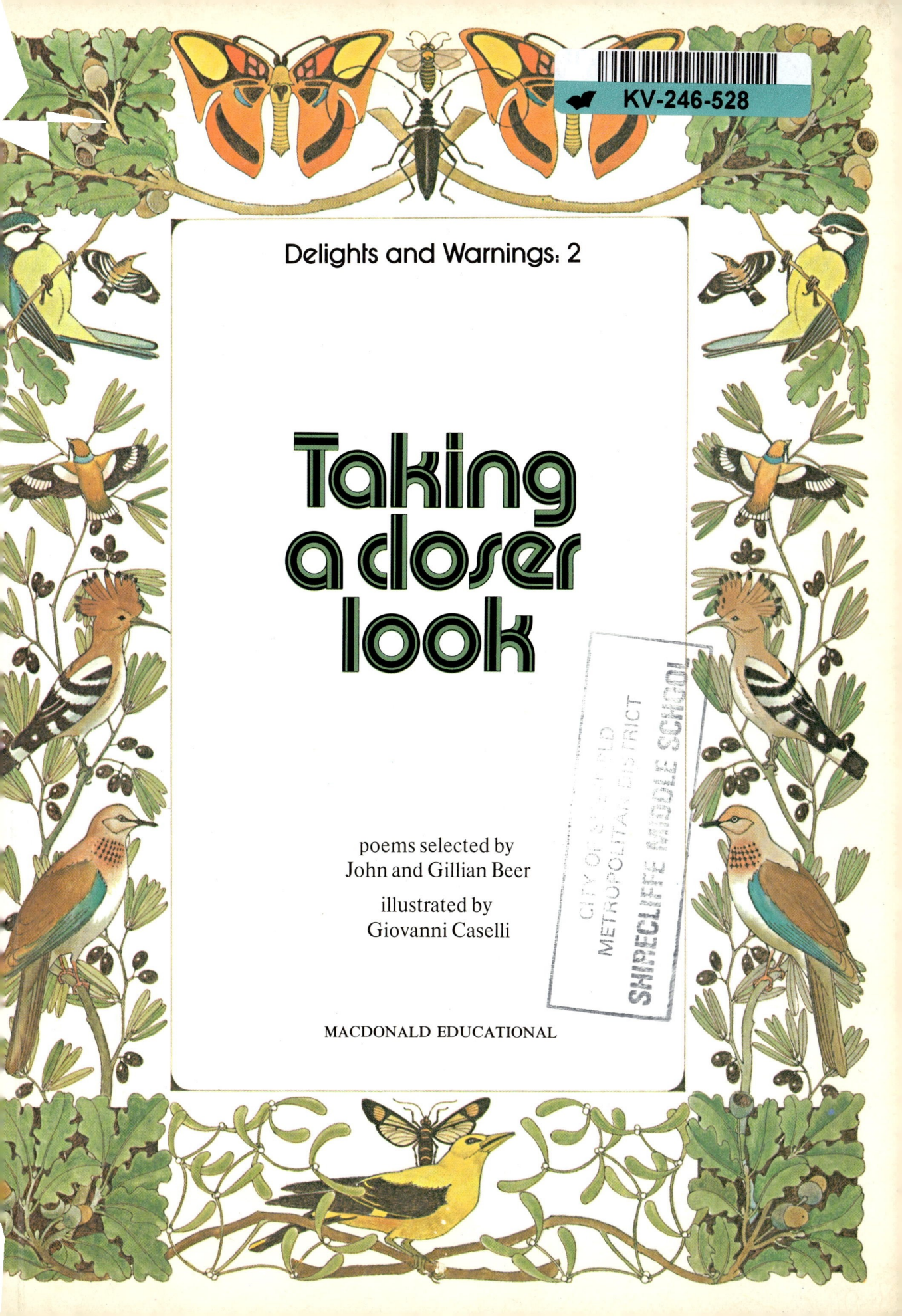

# About the poems

Have you ever tried to describe an animal so that someone else can see exactly what it looks like? You will find it is almost as difficult as trying to describe another human being.

People often use comparisons with animals when talking about a person, and an animal may seem to have human characteristics. Even plants can be given human qualities—like the flowers in the poem **Lodged**.

The first poem in this section, **The Pasture**, is addressed by a grown-up to a child. The poet is trying to be reassuring, as if he knows that the child is probably a bit scared. And in the next poem, **Madam**, we see what it was that the child might have been scared of. The poet here looks back to his childhood, and remembers the terror and delight of having a new large animal about and how it changed things.

Ted Hughes, on the other hand, in **A March Calf**, tries to get right inside a young calf to show us how it might be feeling. At the same time he makes sure that we never stop looking at it as it really is—down to the last little quiver.

**The Bear** is a different kind of poem. The poet does not try to get inside the bear; he just watches him, trying to make us see exactly how he moves. Each time he uses a different way of describing the bear's movement—do you see what they are? And what does the bear seem to think of him?

**The Hedgehog** is different again: we are almost entirely outside the animal, and yet the poet makes us feel affection for him. Can you see how he does it?

John Wain's poem **The Gorilla** describes a gorilla in a cage and this time makes us think of him as if he were a man. What kind of man do you think he is though? A labouring man? A strong man? You might think so from the second stanza, but now look at the last two.

John Wain's gorilla is seen as a lazy animal; whereas **Weary Will** the wombat, who sounds from his name like a lazy animal, is about the most active animal in any of these poems, even though he only does one thing all the time.

Now look at the two poems describing lizards (**Gecko** and **The Lizard**). Which do you like best? Do you think one of them is better at showing what a lizard is really like?

**Sea-weed** and **Little Fish** are both by D. H. Lawrence. Notice how he says just one thing to catch the look of seaweed and one thing to describe the life of small fish in the sea. Can you write a short poem like that, saying just one thing about something to bring it alive?

It is not difficult to think of animals as being like humans, but when it comes to snails and worms you might think it was almost impossible.

**Snails** shows us one way in which snails are definitely not like us. Do you agree that it would be better if human beings were made this way?

In the case of worms we don't have to ask this question; although **Worms and the Wind** is about worms, it is much more about people. In what ways do we all behave like these worms?

**The Fly** looks at the way the world must seem to a small insect. **Serious Readers** on the other hand, looks at the way flies seem to us.

Now imagine yourself the size of Tom Thumb and you will understand how the tiny Lilliputian feels in **A Poem to Gulliver**. His view of Gulliver sounds just amusing—but it also shows how we sometimes respect things or people only because they are bigger than us.

If we had the senses of a tiny animal, we would hear things we don't usually hear as human beings. The man in **Lost Love** is seeing and hearing in this way, because he is so eager to find what he has lost. Reading the poem is rather like watching a film in which every tiny detail is magnified to many times its normal size.

This section includes a number of poems about the countryside and the way we look at it. In the past, country people were often looking for signs of the weather. They have handed down some of their best tips as little rhymes that are easy to remember. Of these, perhaps **Red Sky at Night** works best as a poem, because all the important words come in just the right places.

Of course we also go into the countryside to enjoy ourselves. Thomas Hardy's **Weathers** tries to get the feel of different kinds of weather by using very small details. In **The Spring** and **The Waking** too, we remember what it is like to go outside on a bright sunny day when the countryside seems as happy as we are.

In winter, the snow often makes everything look the same. But, as David McCord tells us, in **Snowflakes**, if you look at snowflakes under a microscope, no two flakes are the same. The world is full of things that we hardly stop to look at—like the dapples in Hopkins' **Pied Beauty**.

Now think about the first time you tried to ride a bicycle and then read **Esmé on her Brother's Bicycle**. Can you see anything that tells you the sort of girl she is? Poets notice things like this, and are always thinking of ways to describe them and pin them down. Like W. H. Davies, in **Leisure**, they find it worthwhile to stand and stare.

Even on a cold winter's night Robert Frost finds himself stopping to look into a wood. Try reading **Stopping by Woods** aloud, and you will see how often the poem goes on again, just when you think it might come to a stop. How does this help what he is saying?

In the last poem you will see how he sometimes enjoys making his words look awkward. **Neither out Far nor in Deep** is an odd title for a poem—but what he is talking about *is* odd: people by the sea tend to look out to sea rather than back at the land, even though there's much less to see.

This is a poem in which we take a closer look at the way other people look at the world—and see that this is sometimes much stranger than anything else that they, or we, are ever likely to see.

## THE PASTURE

I'm going out to clean the pasture spring;
I'll only stop to rake the leaves away
(And wait to watch the water clear, I may):
I shan't be gone long.—You come too.

I'm going out to fetch the little calf
That's standing by the mother. It's so young,
It totters when she licks it with her tongue.
I shan't be gone long.—You come too.

ROBERT FROST

## MADAM

One day grandfather came home with a calf
on a lead, grinning with his milk-white teeth.
Immediately we named her Madam, her hooves
clicked so much like high-heels in the courtyard.
'She'll give us milk in a year and a half,
and if she doesn't we'll slaughter her for beef,'
said grandfather, tying her under the guava leaves
in the garden. I stared and stared and stared,

and Madam stared back across the flower-bed.
I stood sucking a thumb and clutching the tail
of my nightshirt in the hot afternoon,
always on my toes and ready to run
to mother at the slightest turning of her head.
At evening I carried a bucket of meal
to Madam and with some confidence got within
a foot of touching her, and then I'd run

away carrying the smell of her sweating hide
to my pillow and the smell of her dung.
She would appear in my dreams dyed with red
pigment as for a festival, full grown
cow, her udders swaying from side to side
as she mooned away from the fields I'd hang
about in. The bizarre problems of childhood!
Ballooned in my nightshirt, I dreamed on.

No strategy could make Madam mine
as was the tricycle I rode or the thumb
which was sore with sucking. The dreams were
    hard-luck
stories. While Madam's sides bulged like a pear,
I ate fruit only of imagining,
touched her in thought. Where I went she
    wouldn't come.
Madam kicked me once in the stomach.
I suppose I shouldn't have gone so near.

ZULFIKAR GHOSE

5

# A MARCH CALF

Right from the start he is dressed in his best—his
   blacks and his whites,
Little Fauntleroy—quiffed and glossy,
A Sunday suit, a wedding natty get-up,
Standing in dunged straw

Under cobwebby beams, near the mud wall,
Half of him legs,
Shining-eyed, requiring nothing more
But that mother's milk come back often.

Everything else is in order, just as it is.
Let the summer skies hold off, for the moment.
This is just as he wants it.
A little at a time, of each new thing, is best.

Too much and too sudden is too frightening—
When I block the light, a bulk from space,
To let him in to his mother for a suck,
He bolts a yard or two, then freezes,

Staring from every hair in all directions
Ready for the worst, shut up in his hopeful
   religion,
A little syllogism
With a wet blue-reddish muzzle, for God's thumb.

You see all his hopes bustling
As he reaches between the worn rails towards
The topheavy oven of his mother.
He trembles to grow, stretching his curl-tip
   tongue—

What did cattle ever find here
To make this dear little fellow
So eager to prepare himself?
He is already in the race, and quivering to win—

His new purpled eyeball swivel-jerks
In the elbowing push of his plans.
Hungry people are getting hungrier,
Butchers developing expertise and markets,

But he just wobbles his tail—and glistens
Within his dapper profile
Unaware of how his whole lineage
Has been tied up.

He shivers for feel of the world licking his side.
He is like an ember—one glow
Of lighting himself up
With the fuel of himself, breathing and
    brightening.

Soon he'll plunge out, to scatter his seething joy,
To be present at the grass,
To be free on the surface of such a wideness,
To find himself himself. To stand. To moo.

TED HUGHES

## THE BEAR

His sullen shaggy-rimmed eyes followed my
    every move,
Slowly gyrating they seemed to mimic the
    movements of his massive head.
Similarly his body rolled unceasingly
From within.
As though each part possessed its own motion
And could think
And move for itself alone.
He had come forward in a lumbering, heavy spurt;
Like a beer barrel rolling down a plank.
The tremendous volume of his blood-red mouth
Yawned
So casually
But with so much menace.
And still the eye held yours.
So that you had to stay.
And then it turned.
Away.
So slowly.
Back
With that same motion
Back
To the bun-strewn
And honey-smelling back of its cage.

FREDERICK BROWN

## HEDGEHOG

Twitching the leaves just where the drainpipe clogs
In ivy leaves and mud, a purposeful
Creature at night about its business. Dogs
Fear his stiff seriousness. He chews away

At beetles, worms, slugs, frogs. Can kill a hen
With one snap of his jaws, can taunt a snake
To death on muscled spines. Old countrymen
Tell tales of hedgehogs sucking a cow dry.

But this one, cramped by houses, fences, walls,
Must have slept here all winter in that heap
Of compost, or have inched by intervals
Through tidy gardens to this ivy bed.

And here, dim-eyed, but ears so sensitive
A voice within the house can make him freeze,
He scuffs the edge of danger: yet can live
Happily in our nights and absences.

A country creature, wary, quiet and shrewd,
He takes the milk we give him, when we're gone.
At night, our slamming voices must seem crude
To one who sits and waits for silences.

ANTHONY THWAITE

## THE GORILLA

The gorilla lay on his back,
One hand cupped under his head,
Like a man.

Like a labouring man, tired with work,
A strong man with his strength burnt away
In the toil of earning a living.

Only of course he was not tired out with work,
Merely with boredom: his terrible strength
All burnt away by prodigal idleness.

A thousand days, and then a thousand days,
Idleness licked away his beautiful strength,
He having no need to earn a living.

It was all laid on, free of charge.
We maintained him, not for doing anything,
But for being what he was.

And so that Sunday morning he lay on his back,
Like a man, like a worn-out man,
One hand cupped under his terrible hard head.

Like a man, like a man,
One of those we maintain, not for doing anything,
But for being what they are.

A thousand days, and then a thousand days,
With everything laid on, free of charge,
They cup their heads in prodigal idleness.

JOHN WAIN
'*Au Jardin des Plantes*'

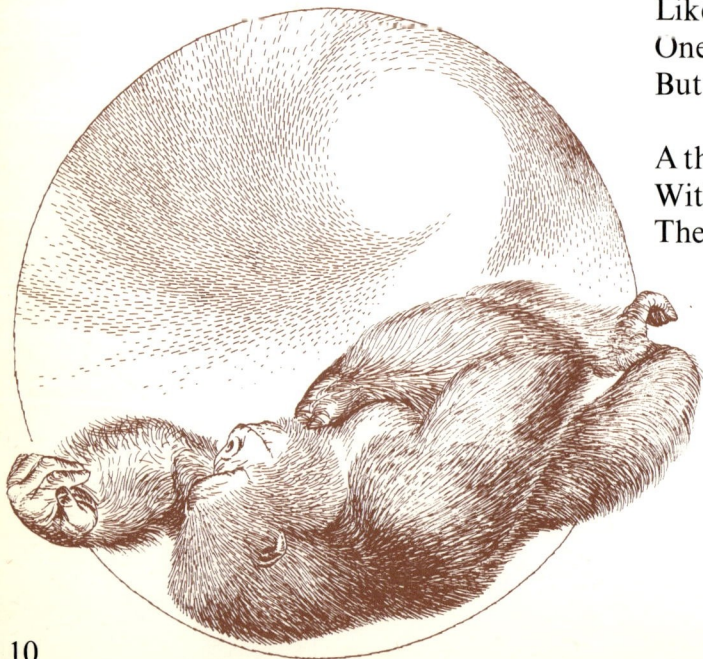

# WEARY WILL

The strongest creature for his size
But least equipped for combat
That dwells beneath Australian skies
Is Weary Will the Wombat.

He digs his homestead underground,
He's neither shrewd nor clever;
For kangaroos can leap and bound
But wombats dig for ever.

The boundary-rider's netting fence
Excites his irritation;
It is to his untutored sense
His pet abomination.

And when to pass it he desires,
Upon his task he'll centre
And dig a hole beneath the wires,
Through which the dingoes enter.

And when to block the hole they strain
With logs and stones and rubble,
Bill Wombat digs it out again
Without the slightest trouble.

The boundary-rider bows to fate,
Admits he's made a blunder,
And rigs a little swinging gate
To let Bill Wombat under.

So most contentedly he goes
Between his haunt and burrow:
He does the only thing he knows,
And does it very thorough.

A. B. PATERSON

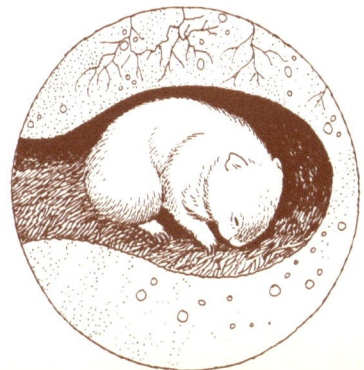

11

# GECKO

There was a lizard kept me company
when I was in Gozo in the summer heat;
*Gecko*, they said he was—but to me
a lizard, fast, fleet—
'He'll bring you luck,' they told me.

Swift, pretty creature, my luck
was to have you there at all,
to watch you, now still as stone
then—a flick, a flip, and you were gone
fast as fury up the whitewashed wall,—
fly-prey snatched by your whip-crack tongue.

I loved your scaly pre-historic old-man's-face
with bulging eyes—pinpoints of light;
your suckered feet on plump doll's legs;
your tail, a graceful question mark.

Gecko, entrancing guest, you brought
an ancient beauty to my bare white wall.

NOEL LLOYD

## THE LIZARD

He too has eaten well—
I can see that by the distended pulsing middle;
And his world and mine are the same,
The Mediterranean sun shining on us, equally,
His head, stiff as a scarab, turned to one side,
His right eye staring straight at me,
One leaf-like foot hung laxly
Over the worn curb of the terrace,
The tail straight as an awl,
Then suddenly flung up and over,
Ending curled around and over again,
A thread-like firmness.

(Would a cigarette disturb him?)

At the first scratch of the match
He turns his head slightly,
Retiring to nudge his neck half-way under
A dried strawberry leaf,
His tail grey with the ground now,
One round eye still toward me.
A white cabbage-butterfly drifts in,
Bumbling up and around the bamboo windbreak;
But the eye of the tiny lizard stays with me.
One greenish lid lifts a bit higher,
Then slides down over the eye's surface,
Rising again, slowly,
Opening, closing.

To whom does this terrace belong?—
With its limestone crumbling into fine greyish
    dust,
Its bevy of bees, and its wind-beaten rickety
    sun-chairs.
Not to me, but this lizard,
Older than I, or the cockroach.

THEODORE ROETHKE

13

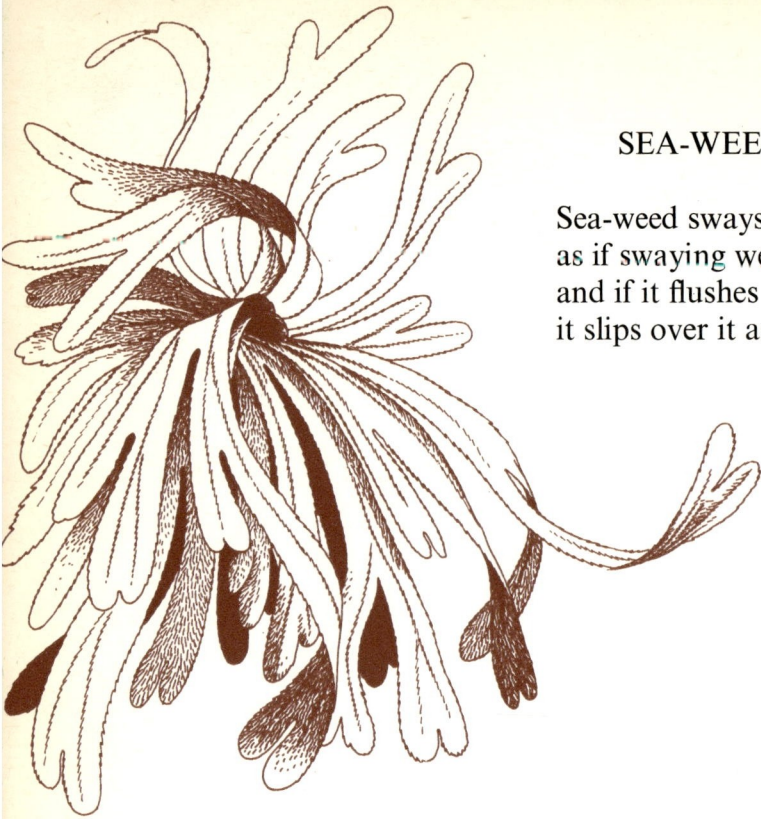

## SEA-WEED

Sea-weed sways and sways and swirls
as if swaying were its form of stillness;
and if it flushes against fierce rock
it slips over it as shadows do, without hurting itself.

D. H. LAWRENCE

## LITTLE FISH

The tiny fish enjoy themselves
in the sea
Quick little splinters of life,
their little lives are fun to them
in the sea.

D. H. LAWRENCE

## THE BABY BLACKBIRD

With head lolling on its fat body,
The baby dozed in sleepy sunlight,
   A few downy feathers,
Like thistle seeds, waving aimlessly in the wind.

The snake-skin eye-lids, like a pelican's great beak,
   Covered the beady eyes:
But as a pigeon cooed lazily,
One lid revealed a deep blue pool of curiosity,
Which was concealed again after one bored blink.

The bird rocked precariously,
Then wobbled over the edge of the fence
Deflated, on the grass, with fast heart-beat,
It tottered unsteadily to its skeleton feet.

CHRISTINE
*aged 15*

## LODGED

The rain to the wind said,
'You push and I'll pelt.'
They so smote the garden bed
That the flowers actually knelt,
And lay lodged—though not dead.
I know how the flowers felt.

ROBERT FROST

## SNAILS

Snails are hermaphrodite
(Which doesn't mean they hunt at night
Or that baby snails are excessively fat
No, it doesn't mean anything like that)
It means something like this;
    First they kiss
        Then they mate
            Then they separate
                Then they BOTH reproduce
To some people this idea may be new
But I can vouch it's perfectly true
If only God had had the foresight
To make us all hermaphrodite!

DOMINIC HODGKIN
*aged 12*

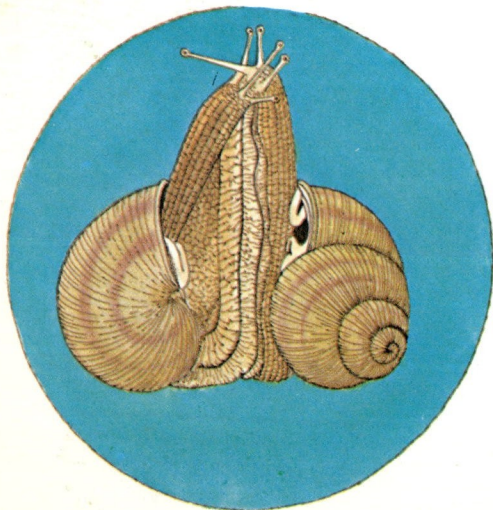

16

## WORMS AND THE WIND

Worms would rather be worms.
Ask a worm and he says, 'Who knows what a
    worm knows?'
Worms go down and up and over and under.
Worms like tunnels.
When worms talk they talk about the worm world.
Worms like it in the dark.
Neither the sun nor the moon interests a worm.
Zigzag worms hate circle worms.
Curve worms never trust square worms.
Worms know what worms want.
Slide worms are suspicious of crawl worms.
One worm asks another, 'How does your belly
    drag today?'
The shape of a crooked worm satisfies a crooked
    worm.
A straight worm says, 'Why not be straight?'
Worms tired of crawling begin to slither.
Long worms slither farther than short worms.
Middle-sized worms say, 'It is nice to be neither
    long nor short.'
Old worms teach young worms to say, 'Don't be
    sorry for me unless you have been a worm and
    lived in worm places and read worm books.'
When worms go to war they dig in, come out and
    fight, dig in again, come out and fight again,
    dig in again, and so on.
Worms underground never hear the wind
    overground and sometimes they ask, 'What is
    this wind we hear of?'

CARL SANDBURG

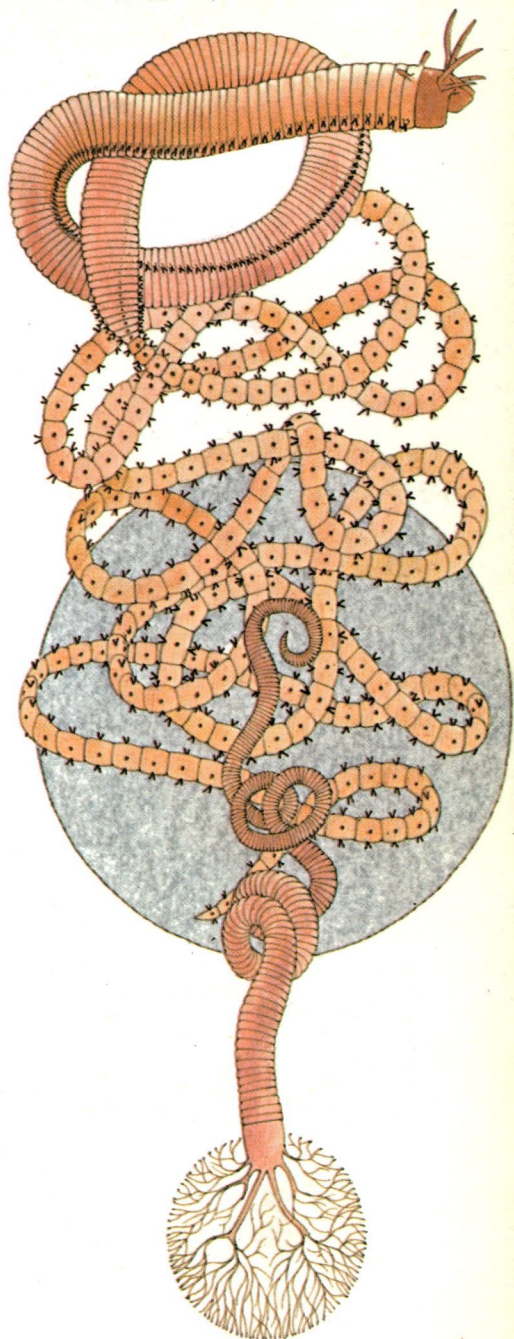

17

## THE FLY

How large unto the tiny fly
   Must little things appear!—
A rosebud like a feather bed,
   Its prickle like a spear;

A dewdrop like a looking-glass,
   A hair like golden wire;
The smallest grain of mustard-seed
   As fierce as coals of fire;

A loaf of bread, a lofty hill;
   A wasp, a cruel leopard;
And specks of salt as bright to see
   As lambkins to a shepherd.

WALTER DE LA MARE

18

## SERIOUS READERS

All the flies are reading microscopic books;
They hold themselves quite tense and silent
With shoulders hunched, legs splayed out
On the white formica table-top, reading.
With my book I slide into the diner-booth;
They rise and circle and settle again, reading
With hunched corselets. They do not attempt
    to taste
Before me my fat hamburger-plate, but wait,
Like courteous readers until I put it to one side,
Then taste briefly and resume their tomes
Like reading-stands with horny specs. I
Read as I eat, one fly
Alights on my book, the size of print;
I let it be. Read and let read.

PETER REDGROVE

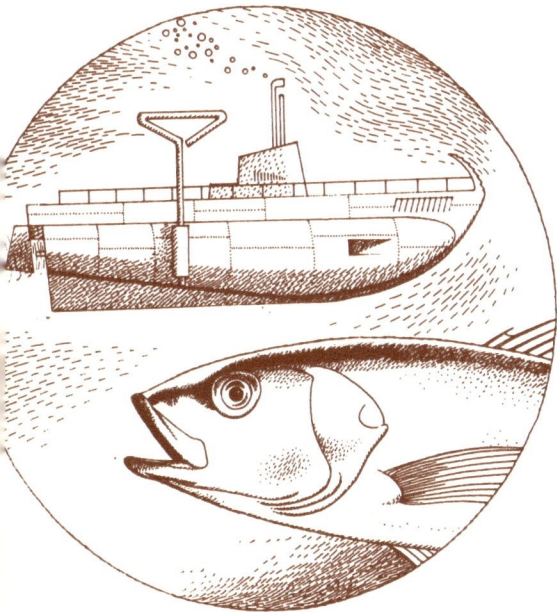

## SARDINES

A baby sardine
Saw her first submarine:
She was scared and watched through a peephole.

'Oh, come, come, come,'
Said the sardine's mum,
'It's only a tin full of people.'

SPIKE MILLIGAN

## A LILLIPUTIAN WRITES
## A POEM TO GULLIVER

See! and believe your Eyes!

See him stride
Vallies wide:
Over Woods,
Over Floods.
When he treads,
Mountains Heads
Groan and shake;
Armies quake,
Lest his Spurn
Overturn
Man and Steed:
Troops take Heed!
Left and Right,
Speed your Flight!
Lest an Host
Beneath his Foot be lost.

Turn'd aside
From his Hide,
Safe from Wound
Darts rebound.
From his Nose
Clouds he blows;
When he speaks,
Thunder breaks!
When he eats,
Famine threats;
When he drinks,
*Neptune* shrinks!
Nigh thy Ear,
In Mid Air,
On thy Hand
Let me stand,
So shall I,
Lofty Poet! touch the Sky.

ALEXANDER POPE
*from 'Verses on
Gulliver's Travels'*

20

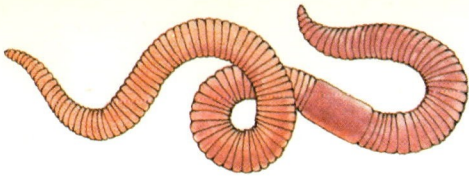

## LOST LOVE

His eyes are quickened so with grief,
He can watch a grass or leaf
Every instant grow; he can
Clearly through a flint wall see,
Or watch the startled spirit flee
From the throat of a dead man.

   Across two counties he can hear,
And catch your words before you speak.
The woodlouse, or the maggot's weak
Clamour rings in his sad ear;
And noise so slight it would surpass
Credence:—drinking sound of grass,
Worm talk, clashing jaws of moth
Chumbling holes in cloth:
The groan of ants who undertake
Gigantic loads for honour's sake,
Their sinews creak, their breath comes thin:
Whir of spiders when they spin,
And minute whispering, mumbling, sighs
Of idle grubs and flies.

   This man is quickened so with grief,
He wanders god-like or like thief
Inside and out, below, above,
Without relief seeking lost love.

ROBERT GRAVES

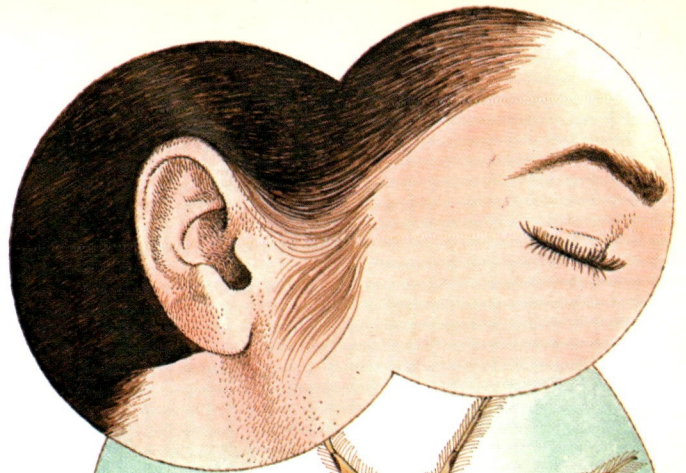

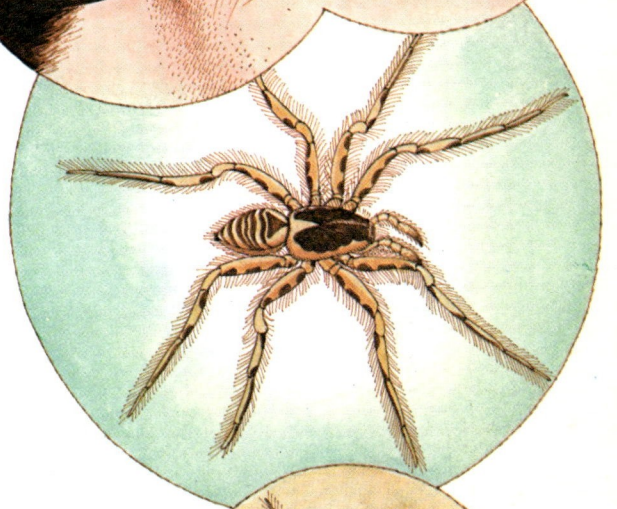

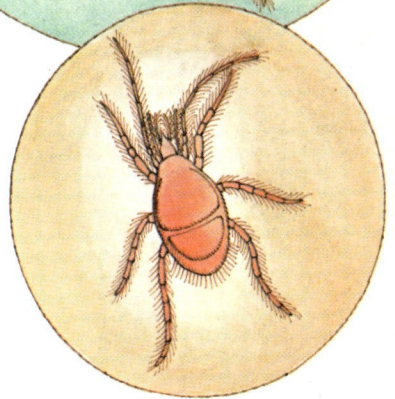

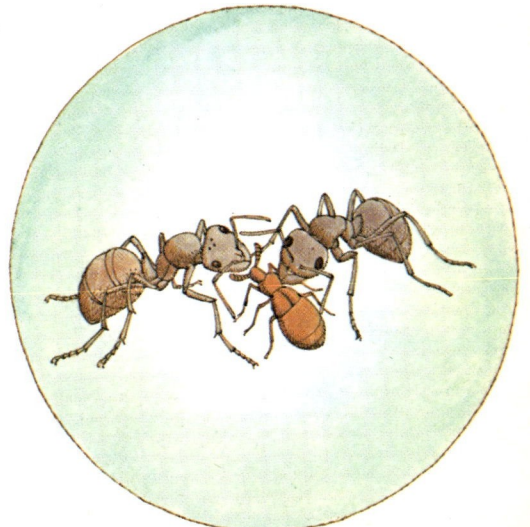

# THE WEATHER FORECAST

Rain, rain, go away,
Come again another day—
Not a public holiday!

Red sky at night,
Shepherd's delight;
Red sky in the morning,
Shepherd's warning.

When clouds appear
Like rocks and towers,
The earth's refreshed
By frequent showers.

Evening red and morning grey
Send the traveller on his way;
Evening grey and morning red
Bring the rain upon his head.

When the wind is in the east,
It's good for neither man nor beast;
When the wind is in the north,
The fisherman he goes not forth;
When the wind is in the south,
It blows the bait in the fishes' mouth;
When the wind is in the west,
Then it's at the very best.

When the dew is on the grass,
Rain will never come to pass.

## WEATHERS

This is the weather the cuckoo likes,
    And so do I;
When showers betumble the chestnut spikes,
    And nestlings fly:
And the little brown nightingale bills his best,
And they sit outside at 'The Travellers' Rest',
And maids come forth sprig-muslin drest,
And citizens dream of the south and west,
    And so do I.

This is the weather the shepherd shuns,
    And so do I;
When beeches drip in browns and duns,
    And thresh, and ply;
And hill-hid tides throb, throe on throe,
And meadow rivulets overflow,
And drops on gate-bars hang in a row,
And rooks in families homeward go,
    And so do I.

THOMAS HARDY

## THE SPRING

Now that the Winter's gone, the earth hath lost
Her snow-white robes; and now no more the frost
Candies the grass, or casts an icy cream
Upon the silver lake or crystal stream:
But the warm sun thaws the benumbed earth,
And makes it tender; gives a sacred birth
To the dead swallow; wakes in hollow tree
The drowsy cuckoo and the humble bee.
Now do a choir of chirping minstrels bring
In triumph to the world the youthful Spring:
The valleys, hills, and woods in rich array
Welcome the coming of the longed-for May.

THOMAS CAREW

## THE WAKING

I strolled across
An open field;
The sun was out;
Heat was happy.

This way! This way!
The wren's throat shimmered,
Either to other,
The blossoms sang.

The stones sang,
The little ones did,
And flowers jumped
Like small goats.

A ragged fringe
Of daisies waved;
I wasn't alone
In a grove of apples.

Far in the wood
A nestling sighed;
The dew loosened
Its morning smells.

I came where the river
Ran over stones:
My ears knew
An early joy.

And all the waters
Of all the streams
Sang in my veins
That summer day.

THEODORE ROETHKE

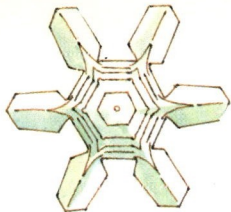

## SNOWFLAKES

Sometime this winter if you go
To walk in soft new-falling snow
When flakes are big and come down slow

To settle on your sleeve as bright
As stars that couldn't wait for night
You won't know what you have in sight—

Another world—unless you bring
A magnifying glass. This thing
We call a snowflake is the king

Of crystals. Do you like surprise?
Examine him three times his size:
At first you won't believe your eyes.

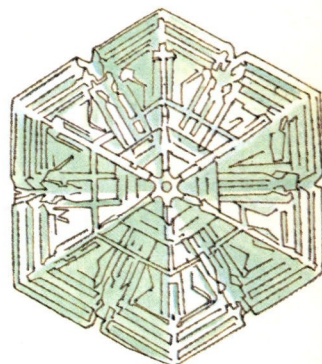

Stars look alike, but flakes do not:
No two the same in all the lot
That you will get in any spot

You chance to be, for every one
Come spinning through the sky has none
But his own window-wings of sun:

Joints, points, and crosses. What could make
Such lacework with no crack or break?
In billion billions, no mistake?

DAVID McCORD

25

## OBITUARY ON THE DEMOLITION OF A HOUSE IN GROVE LANE, CAMBERWELL

On the first day
I saw a woman
Dressed in a jumble sale
Eating a meal at four o'clock
She sat on the steps
And I felt sorry for her
And the house.

On the second day
There were no windows
And in place of a roof
A dull, grey sky:
The men had come
To demolish.

On the third day
It was a hollow shell,
The wall-paper brown-stained
Torn and peeling
Could be seen by all
—But no-one stopped to look.

On the fourth day
There was smoke in the air
Dust around us
The stone crashed around us
And there were men with dirty faces
And it went.

Today
It was a hole
I stopped to see
The sand and rotten wood :
The broken bricks
And solemn cavity
That was once a house.
But no-one seemed concerned.

MARIA DAWSON
*aged 15*

26

## THE DESERTED HOUSE

There's no smoke in the chimney,
   And the rain beats on the floor;
There's no glass in the window,
   There's no wood in the door;
The heather grows behind the house,
   And the sand lies before.

No hand hath trained the ivy,
   The walls are gray and bare;
The boats upon the sea sail by,
   Nor ever tarry there.
No beast of the field comes nigh,
   Nor any bird of the air.

MARY COLERIDGE

## AFTER SPENDING A NIGHT ALONE, AT THE COTTAGE OF A CERTAIN MR. WANG AT PO-SHAN

   Hungry rats race around my bed;
   Bats tumble and dance in lamplight.
Upon the roof, among the pines, wind spouts
incessant rain
While tattered paper flaps against the window,
talks to itself.

   North of the border, south of the Yangtze, no
   stranger to me;
   Now I am home, grey haired, ashen faced —
Cotton quilt, autumn night, and I lie awake;
Ten thousand miles of rivers and hills pass before
my eyes.

HSIN CH'I-CHI

## LEISURE

What is this life if, full of care,
We have no time to stand and stare?

No time to stand beneath the boughs
And stare as long as sheep or cows.

No time to see, when woods we pass,
Where squirrels hide their nuts in grass.

No time to see, in broad daylight,
Streams full of stars, like skies at night.

No time to turn at Beauty's glance,
And watch her feet, how they can dance.

No time to wait till her mouth can
Enrich that smile her eyes began.

A poor life this if, full of care,
We have no time to stand and stare.

WILLIAM H. DAVIES

## ESMÉ ON HER BROTHER'S BICYCLE

One foot on, one foot pushing, Esmé starting off beside
Wheels too tall to mount astride,
Swings the off leg forward featly,
Clears the high bar nimbly, neatly,
With a concentrated frown
Bears the upper pedal down
As the lower rises, then
Brings her whole weight round again,
Leaning forward, gripping tight,
With her knuckles showing white,
Down the road goes, fast and small,
Never sitting down at all.

RUSSELL HOBAN

## PIED BEAUTY

Glory be to God for dappled things—
    For skies of couple-colour as a brinded cow;
      For rose-moles all in stipple upon trout that swim;
Fresh-firecoal chestnut-falls; finches' wings;
    Landscape plotted and pieced—fold, fallow, and plough;
      And all trades, their gear and tackle and trim.

All things counter, original, spare, strange;
    Whatever is fickle, freckled (who knows how?)
      With swift, slow; sweet, sour; adazzle, dim;
He fathers-forth whose beauty is past change:
        Praise him.

GERARD MANLEY HOPKINS

30

## STOPPING BY WOODS
## ON A SNOWY EVENING

Whose woods these are I think I know.
His house is in the village though;
He will not see me stopping here
To watch his woods fill up with snow.

My little horse must think it queer
To stop without a farmhouse near
Between the woods and frozen lake
The darkest evening of the year.

He gives his harness bells a shake
To ask if there is some mistake.
The only other sound's the sweep
Of easy wind and downy flake.

The woods are lovely, dark and deep.
But I have promises to keep,
And miles to go before I sleep,
And miles to go before I sleep.

ROBERT FROST

## NEITHER OUT FAR NOR IN DEEP

The people along the sand
All turn and look one way.
They turn their back on the land.
They look at the sea all day.

As long as it takes to pass
A ship keeps raising its hull;
The wetter ground like glass
Reflects a standing gull.

The land may vary more;
But wherever the truth may be—
The water comes ashore,
And the people look at the sea.

They cannot look out far.
They cannot look in deep.
But when was that ever a bar
To any watch they keep?

ROBERT FROST